Shapes

Seed Learning

circle

square

triangle

rectangle

star

diamond

heart

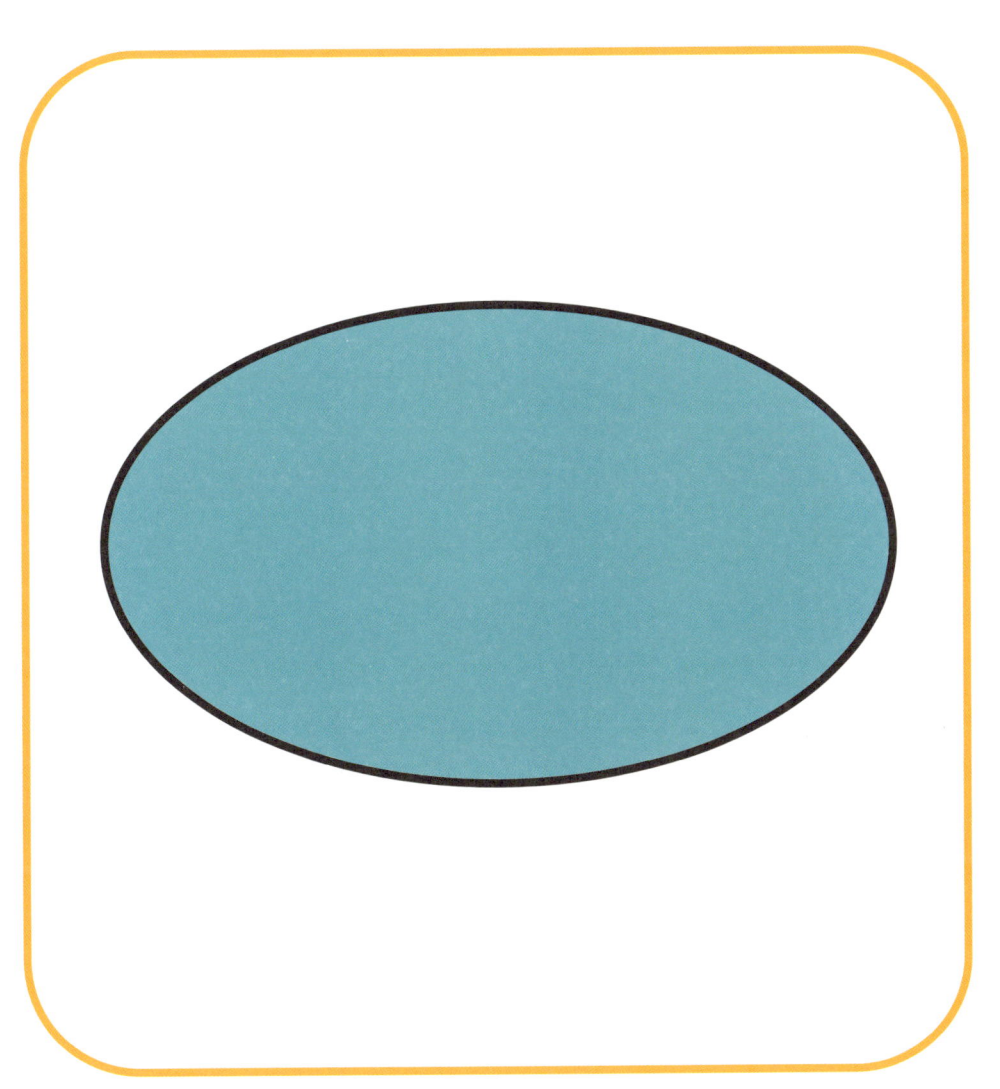

oval

What shape is it?

It's a circle.

What shape is it?

It's a square.

Sun	Mon	Tue	Wed	Thu	Fri	Sat
						1
2	3	4	5	6	7	8
9	10	11	12	13	14	15
16	17	18	19	20	21	22
23	24	25	26	27	28	29
30	31					

What shape is it?

It's a rectangle.

Word List

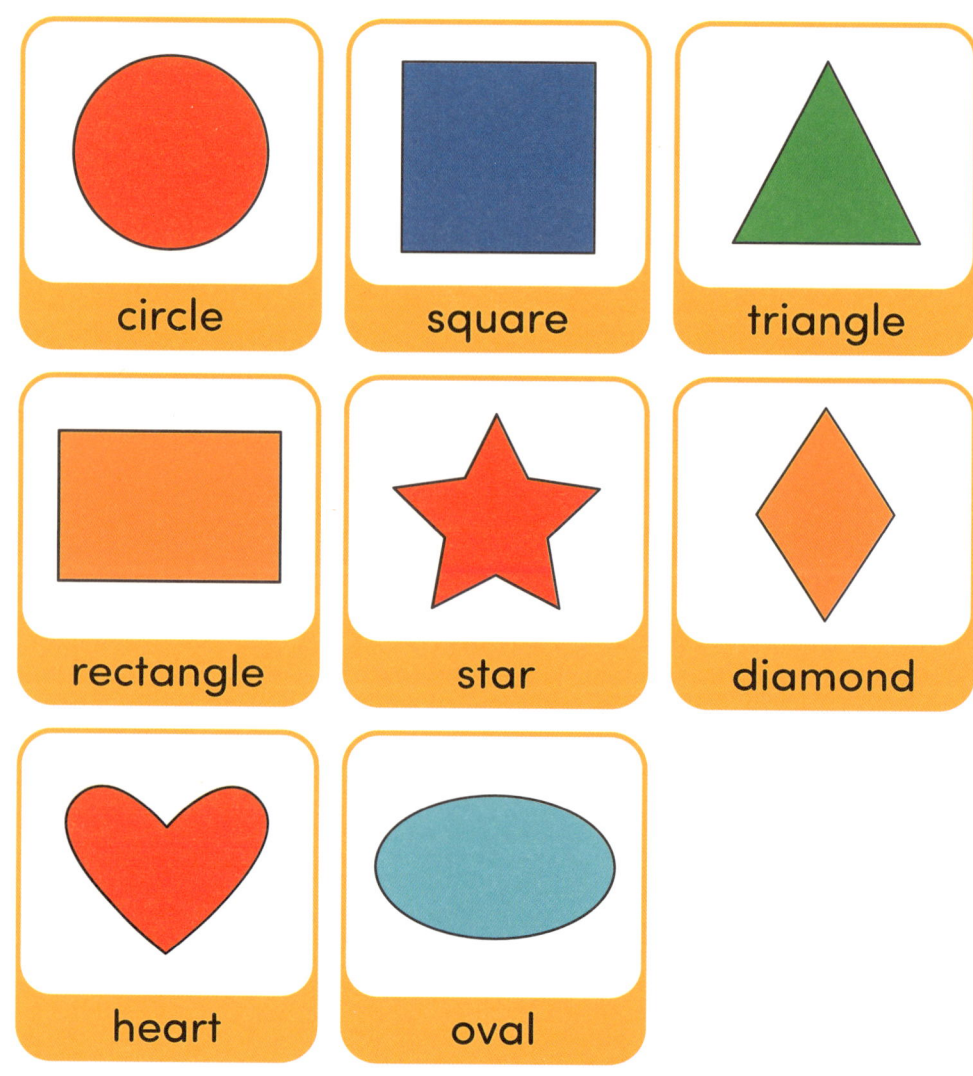

circle

square

triangle

rectangle

star

diamond

heart

oval